HowExpert P

How To Protect Your Personal Computer

Your Step By Step Guide To Protecting Your Personal Computer

HowExpert

For more tips related to this topic, visit HowExpert.com/protectcomputer.

Recommended Resources

- HowExpert.com – Quick 'How To' Guides on All Topics from A to Z by Everyday Experts.
- HowExpert.com/free – Free HowExpert Email Newsletter.
- HowExpert.com/books – HowExpert Books
- HowExpert.com/courses – HowExpert Courses
- HowExpert.com/clothing – HowExpert Clothing
- HowExpert.com/membership – HowExpert Membership Site
- HowExpert.com/affiliates – HowExpert Affiliate Program
- HowExpert.com/writers – Write About Your #1 Passion/Knowledge/Expertise & Become a HowExpert Author.
- HowExpert.com/resources – Additional HowExpert Recommended Resources
- YouTube.com/HowExpert – Subscribe to HowExpert YouTube.
- Instagram.com/HowExpert – Follow HowExpert on Instagram.
- Facebook.com/HowExpert – Follow HowExpert on Facebook.

Publisher's Foreword

Dear HowExpert reader,

HowExpert publishes quick 'how to' guides on all topics from A to Z by everyday experts.

At HowExpert, our mission is to discover, empower, and maximize talents of everyday people to ultimately make a positive impact in the world for all topics from A to Z...one everyday expert at a time!

All of our HowExpert guides are written by everyday people just like you and me who have a passion, knowledge, and expertise for a specific topic.

We take great pride in selecting everyday experts who have a passion, great writing skills, and knowledge about a topic that they love to be able to teach you about the topic you are also passionate about and eager to learn about.

We hope you get a lot of value from our HowExpert guides and it can make a positive impact in your life in some kind of way. All of our readers including you altogether help us continue living our mission of making a positive impact in the world for all spheres of influences from A to Z.

If you enjoyed one of our HowExpert guides, then please take a moment to send us your feedback from wherever you got this book.

Thank you and we wish you all the best in all aspects of life.

Sincerely,

BJ Min
Founder & Publisher of HowExpert
HowExpert.com

PS...If you are also interested in becoming a HowExpert author, then please visit our website at HowExpert.com/writers. Thank you & again, all the best!

Table of Contents

Chapter 1: Introduction

Malware

Malware stands for malicious software. This type of software is designed to secretly access the user's information without his consent.

It is a broader term that covers numerous different types of problematic software.

Some of the more common ones follow:

- Viruses
- Worms
- Trojan Horses
- Spyware
- Adware
- CrimeWare
- KeyLoggers
- Hijackers
- Rogue Security Software

Spyware

Spyware is a type of malware that is stealthily installed on computers. It gathers information about the person and his or her organization through an internet connection.

Some of the most well-known (in some cases because they are the most disastrous)

Types of spyware are as follows:

- Adware
- Snoop Ware
- Browser Hijackers
- Key Loggers
- Dialers
- Trojan Horses
- Cookies

Viruses

Viruses are reproducing software programs that can copy themselves onto your computer system and cause great damage to files and other programs.

The most common types of viruses are as follows:

- Resident Viruses
- Direct Action Viruses
- Overwrite Viruses
- Boot Viruses
- Macro Viruses
- Dictionary Viruses
- Polymorphic Viruses
- FAT Viruses
- Logic Bombs

Chapter 2: What The Guide Focuses On

All types of malicious software affect millions of computer systems every day and cause enormous economic and social damage. Computer malware, spyware and other computer threatening programs behave similarly to biological viruses and worms, and have different destructive effects on computer systems.

This guide will equip the reader with a variety of options, from built-in utilities to paid software to protect your system from suspicious and unwanted malicious programs. It will provide you guidelines to protect your personal computer and perform your routine tasks without any inconvenience.

Chapter 3: How The Computer Becomes Infected

Although computer systems help people in thousands of ways, the computer experience becomes annoying when the suspicious software or viruses affect the computer systems. There are multiple ways in which computers get infected.

Computer system become infected when

- Opening an email attachment from an unknown person.
- Downloading infected application programs or software
- Not using updated software
- Accepting options offered without reading them

Chapter 4: How To Protect Your Personal Computer

This chapter contains some of the best general tactics and built-in utilities to protect your personal computers. These are equally helpful for all versions of Windows OS but may have a few variations in the steps you need to follow depending upon which version you're using.

A complete list of these tactics and their comprehensive details are stated below:

How To Protect Your Files With Passwords

Windows offers a password protection utility to protect the confidential files.

The following steps are involved in making your files password protected:

- Create a Word document and from the **Office button,** click on the **Save As** option.
- From the opening dialog box, Select **Tools** and then navigate to the **General** option**.**

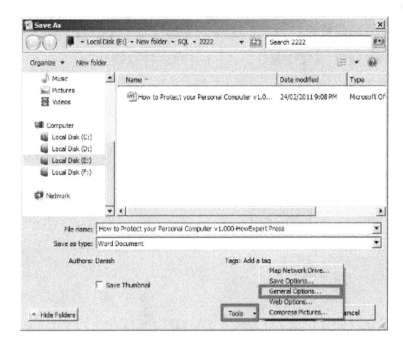

Save As Option

- Enter a password in the field **Password to Open.**
- In the next field, the user can enter another password in the field labeled **Password to Modify** if he/she wants to use the password protection for modifying the file as well.

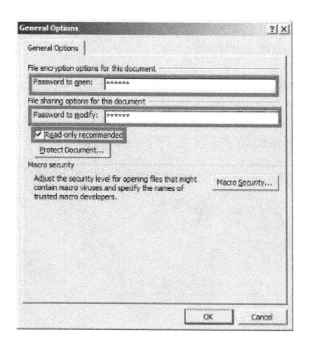

General Option

- If the user wants to make the file available as solely a read only format, then enable the option **Read only Recommended.**
- Click **Ok** to apply the password protection.

How To Use Password Protection for Folders

Windows also offers password protection to individual folders which have confidential material.

Following are the steps to utilize the password protection for folders:

- Right click on the folder that you want to make password protected.
- Select **Properties** and from the opening window, select the **Sharing tab.**

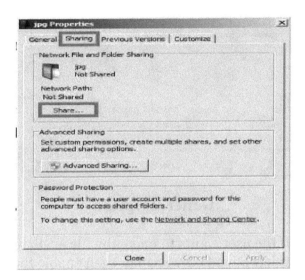

Folder Properties

- The user may select the people who will be able to access the folder by using the option

Choose people to share with.

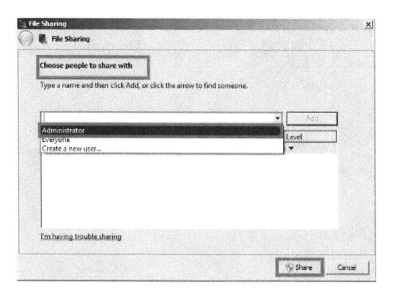

File Sharing

- The user may limit the **Level of Permission** from the same dialog box.
- Click **Share** to apply changes.

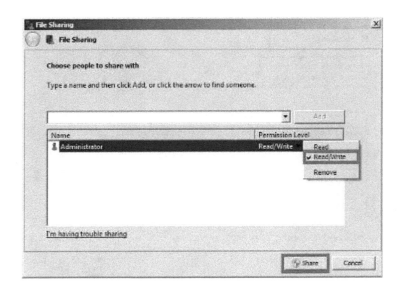

File Sharing Option

Note: In some other operating systems, the user is also offered an option called **Make this Folder Private** to limit the access of folder.

How To Password Protect With WinRAR

WinRAR is a data compression utility that is able to create RAR archives. It is one of the most popular shareware programs and offers a password protection facility to guard both files and folders.

The following steps are required to follow to ensure the safety of files using WinRAR:

- Select **WinRAR** and click on the **Add** option to select the file or folder.
- Click on the **Advanced tab** and select the **Set Password** option.

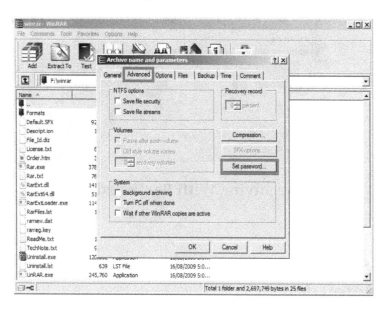

Archive Name And Parameter

- In the next opening window, type the password in the first field labeled **Enter Password** and then reenter the password in the second field for verification.
- User can also encrypt the file by checking the option labeled **Encrypt the file name.**
- Click OK first in the **Archiving with password** window and then the **Achieve name and parameters** windows.

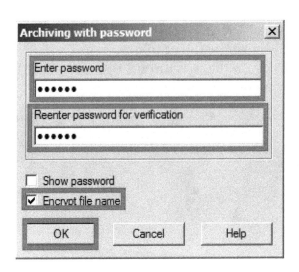

Archiving With Password

How To Activate Windows Defender

Many operating systems have preinstalled the Windows Defender utility to protect the computer system from malicious & unwanted software.

The following steps are required to activate the Windows Defender utility:

- Click on the **Start** button and navigate to the **Control Panel.**
- From the control panel items, click on **Windows Defender.**
- Select the **Tools** tab and then choose **Option.**

Windows Defender

- Select the **Administration** option and check the option **Use this program.**
- Click on the **Save tab** to apply changes.

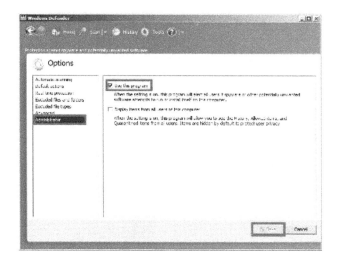

Windows Defender Option

How To Turn On Windows Automatic Update

Windows serves the user by offering the automatic update installation options that also offer the advantages of reliability and improved security.

The user can activate the automatic update option by following the steps below:

- Click on the **Start** button and move to **All Programs.**
- From the appeared list, select **Windows Update** and then click on **Change Settings** from the left panel.

Windows Update Settings

- Under the **Recommended updates**, select the option of your choice to install important updates.
- The user may check the option **Recommended updates** and also decide whether to give the update responsibility to the administrator or to multiple users by selecting the **Who Can Install Updates** option.
- Click **OK.**

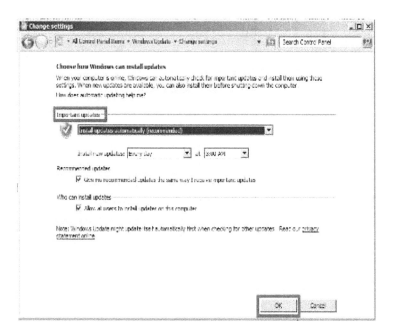

Windows Update Settings

How To Employ A Firewall

A Windows firewall is a preinstalled utility which helps to alert the user if a virus or malware attempts to halt the system.

To enable the Windows firewall is a very simple process which requires only few steps to complete:

- Open the Control Panel and select the Windows Firewall.
- From the left pane of the opening window, select Turn Windows Firewall on or off.
- Under each network location, check the Windows Firewall option to activate it.
- Click OK.

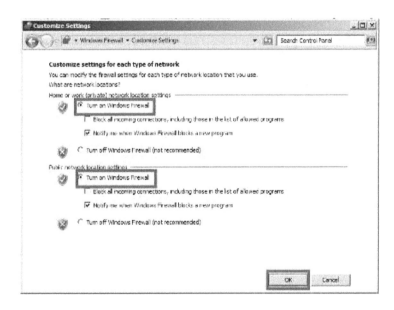

Windows Firewall

Note: Experts suggest turning on firewalls for all network location categories for protecting the computer system.

How To Adjust User Account Control Settings

UAC notifies the user when some program or other form of interference tries to make the changes to your computer system that requires your administrator's consent.

The user can alter the setting for how often UAC warns him by following the steps suggested below:

- Click on the **Start** button and select the **Control Panel.**
- Click on the **User Accounts** icon.
- Select the **Change User Account Settings** option.

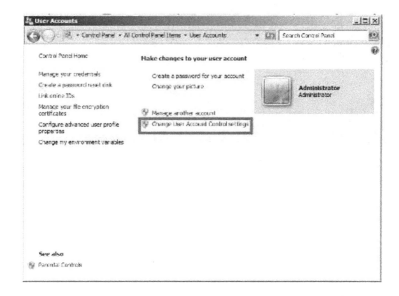

User Account Setting

- The user can change the level of how often he wants the notifications to appear by dragging the slider on either of the sides from **Always notify** to **Never Notify.**
- Click **OK.**

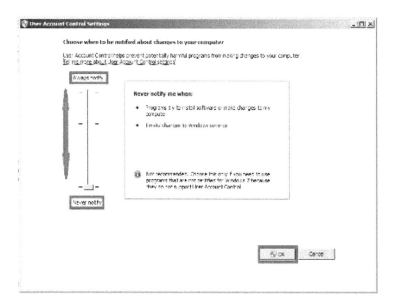

User Account Control Settings

Note: Experts recommend that the user should select the option Always notify or the Default settings if he is using some accessibility device like a screen reader.

How To Perform Internet Browsing And Downloading Carefully

Experts suggest that the best way to prevent spyware, malware and viruses to is to be very careful while surfing or downloading any program.

Some of the most simple but useful instructions on how to do this are listed below:

- Download software only from trusted websites.
- Carefully understand the license agreement, privacy statement and warning that are coupled with the specific software you want to install.
- Never choose OK as an option or agree to close any window. Always click on the cross X placed at the top right corner of all the windows or use the keyboard option Alt+F4 to close the window.
- Be especially careful while downloading free music, movies or games. These sites are frequent breeding grounds for malware.

Do Not Open Suspicious Email Attachments

Many specialists suggest being careful while opening unexpected attachments of emails from unknown persons or email addresses. These unforeseen emails are potentially harmful because many intruders make use of these types of email attachments for illegal and destructive activities.

Chapter 5: How To Adjust Browser Settings To Protect Your PC

Usually, computers get infected when the users have frequent access to the Internet. A user can avoid the potential threats associated with the internet by adjusting internet browser settings to the recommended level. Various web browsers share a few common security settings, with small variation in the steps to be followed.

This chapter contains some of the common and recommended security settings for the most widely used internet browsers like Internet Explorer, Google Chrome, Mozilla Firefox, etc.

How To Adjust Internet Explorer Settings

Internet Explorer is one of the oldest and most widely used search engines, and it has been used for internet surfing by most computer users at one point or another. In fact, there are still sites which only work well with Internet Explorer so even those who primarily use another search engine often keep it around for just that purpose.

Some of the most helpful security settings for Internet Explorer are listed below:

Change Security Settings Of Internet Explorer

A trusted way to secure your computer system from malware and viruses is to set Internet Explorer security settings for **Internet Zone**.

The following steps are involved to set internet security for a secure internet experience:

- Click on the **Internet Explorer** icon placed on the desktop or open it from the **Start** menu.
- Click on **Tools** and select the **Internet Option.**
- Click on the **Security** tab. Here the user can adjust **security settings** by dragging the slider from **Medium to Higher.**
- Click **OK** to apply the changes.

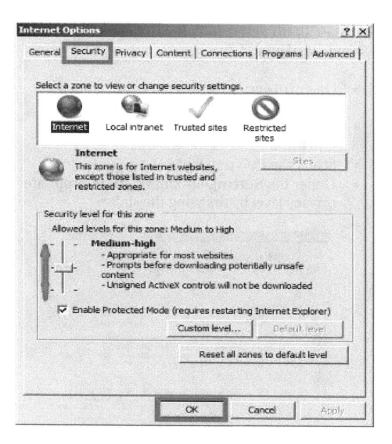

Internet Option

Adjusting Internet Explorer Privacy Settings

The user can employ the Internet Explorer privacy settings to prevent their private information being used for fraud, identity theft, etc.

The user is directed to follow these steps to set privacy settings:

- Open **Internet Explorer,** either from the desktop or from the **Start** button.
- Select **Tools** and then choose **Internet Options.**
- Select the **Privacy** tab.
- Under the **Setting** option, set the appropriate privacy level by dragging the slider.

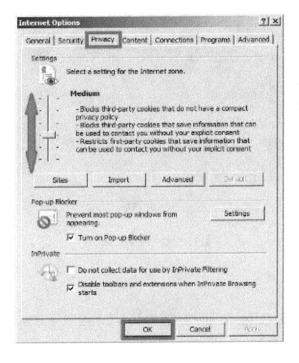

Internet Privacy Option

- The user may block **Pop-up windows** by checking the **Turn on Pop-up blocker** from the same window.

- The user can also enable the **InPrivate** option to prevent websites from automatically sharing the information about your visit.
- Click **OK.**

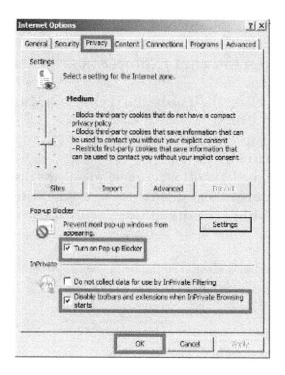

Internet Privacy Options

Adjust Settings To Prevent Modification Of Default Search Provider

User can eliminate the threat of changing the default search provider of internet explorer from the programs by selecting the option "Prevent Programs from Suggesting Changes to my Default Search Provider."

The following steps are involved to activate this particular option:

- Open **Internet Explorer** from the Start menu.
- Click on the **Tools** and then select **Manage add-ons.**
- Below the **Add-on types,** select the option **Search Providers.**
- In the left bottom corner, enable the option **Prevent Programs from suggesting changes to my default search provider.**
- Click the **Close** button.

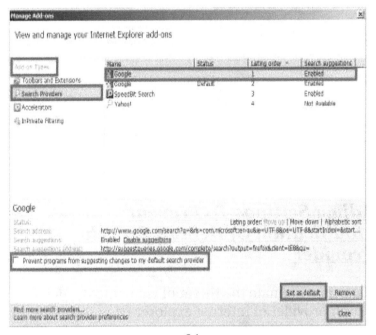

Ensure That Internet Explorer Settings Are At Recommended Levels

The user can also avoid potential threats by ensuring that all Internet Explorer settings are adjusted to the recommended level.

The following steps are involved to determine the level of settings:

- Click on the **Internet Explorer** icon placed on the desktop, or open it from the **Start** menu.
- Click on the button labeled **Tools** and then choose **Internet Option.**
- Select the **Security** tab.
- Click the **Internet** icon and then click on the **Custom Level** Button.

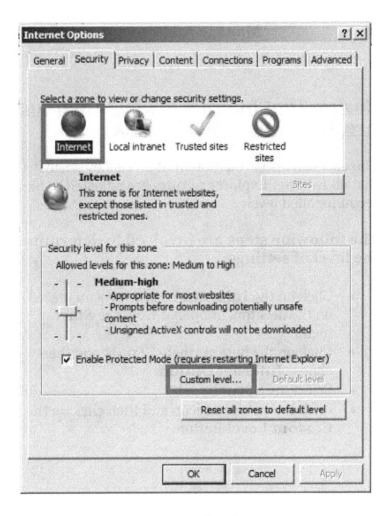

Internet Option

- Settings that are not at recommended levels will be highlighted in red color. Check the options that are labeled **Recommended** within parenthesis for preventing potential threats.
- Click **OK.**

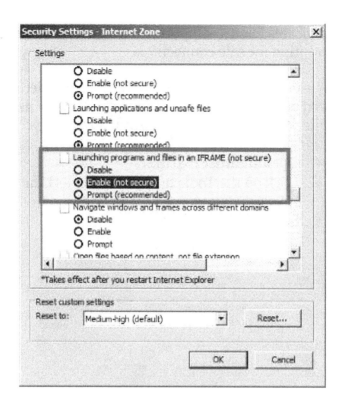

Security Setting-Internet Zone

Adjusting Content Setting In Internet Explorer

The user can also ensure a safe internet experience by making suitable content settings. This browser offers a Parental Control feature that is useful to control what internet content is visible when children are surfing. The Content Adviser tool assists the user to block or allow particular web pages that are decided by the sites' content rating. In addition, the

37

Certificates feature supports identifying websites and encryption for safe connections.

The user can make use of these settings to delete his stored personal security information when he uses a public computer kiosk by following these steps:

- Open Internet Explorer.
- Click on the Tools tab and then select the Internet Option.
- Select the Content tab.

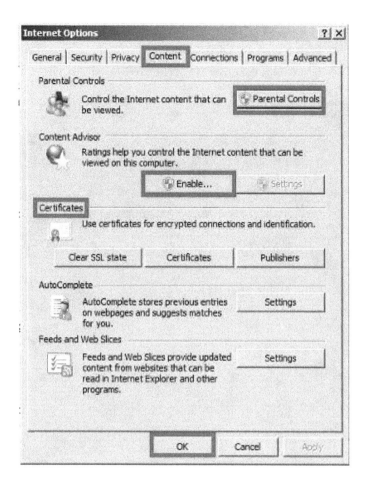

Internet Option

- Click on the **Parental Control** tab and then click on the standard user account for adjusting **parental controls.** Under Parental Control, Click **On.**
- Below the **Content advisor,** select the **Settings** and in the next opening window, enter the URL in the first field labeled **Allow**

this website and then select **Always** or **Never** at your discretion.

- Click **OK** to save the changes.

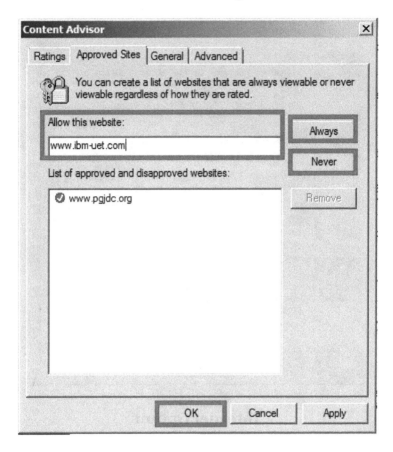

Content Advisor

How To Adjust Security Settings For Mozilla Firefox

Mozilla Firefox is also one of the most well- known internet browsers at the present time. It has many features similar to Internet Explorer. The user can set security settings to the suggested levels by following the tactics listed below:

Set The General Settings

- Select the **Tools** menu and navigate the mouse to the select the **Option.**
- The **Option** window will appear under the **general** tab. Enable the option **Always ask me where to save the file.**

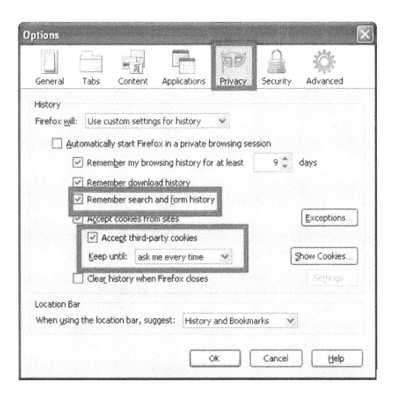

Privacy Settings Window

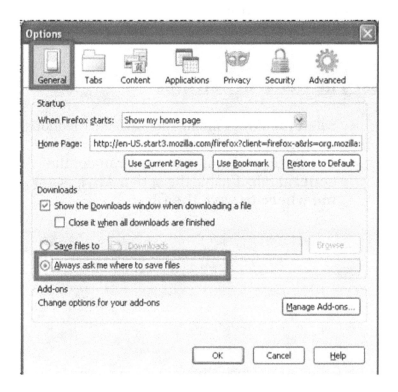

Option Window

- From the same window, click on the **Privacy** tab, and disable the option **Remember search and Form History.** Below the **Accept the third-party Cookies** section, select the option **Ask me every time** to control the confidentiality of your system.

- Now move to the **Security** tab. Check the option **Warn me when sites try to install Add-ons** to alert you. The user can also

employ password protection by using the
option Use a master password.

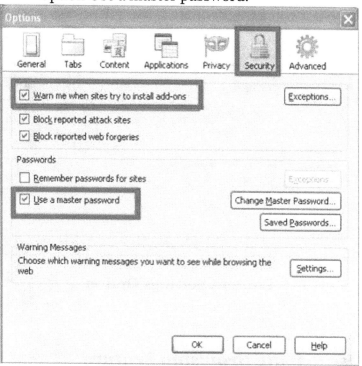

Security Setting Window

- Click on the **Content** tab, and after this
  disable the option **Enable Javascript.**
  Javascript is a programming language and the
  user should enable it only for trusted web sites.
- The user may set advanced settings from this
  same window. For this, click on the **Advanced
  button**. A small dialog box containing 4-5
  options will appear. We suggested that you
  disable all of the options.

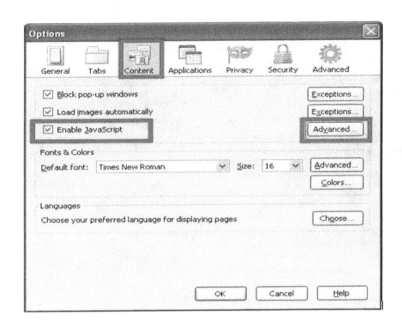

Content Settings Option

Use Private Browsing Feature

Mozilla Firefox offers a highly exhilarating feature called **Private Browsing** to secure your browsing history. It is quick and easy to use.

The user can make use of this feature as stated below:

- Click on the **Tools** menu and click on the **Start Private Browsing** option. A new window will appear. The user can browse anything confidential, such as online bank browsing, while sitting in a private internet café. The browsing history cannot be traced while browsing in this mode.

- The user can go back to normal or the previous mode by simple selecting the option **Stop Private Browsing from the Tools menu.**

Clear Recent Browsing History

Mozilla Firefox has also introduced a simple procedure to clear the browsing history. You have full control to delete the browsing history up to the last few hours and to remove the optional browsing contents like cookies, cache, etc.

Only a few steps are involved to remove the history:

- Go to the **Tools** menu and select **Clear Recent History** Option.
- From the appearing dialog box, expand the first field labeled **Time range to clear** and select the time interval.
- Next, expand the **Details** option by clicking on it. The user may randomly select which web content he/she wants to remove.
- Click on **Clear Now** to remove the selected history.

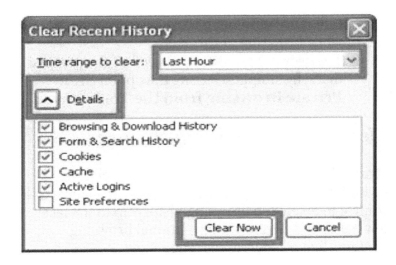

Clear Recent History Option

How To Adjust Security Settings For Google Chrome

Google Chrome is an updated web browser used to quickly launch websites and also supports the feature of searching directly from the address bar.

The following steps are involved to set security measures for Google Chrome:

- Launch **Google Chrome** and click on the **Wrench** icon placed on the browse toolbar.
- From the drop-down list, select **Options.**
- Select the tab labeled **Under the Hood.**
- Under **Security,** check the option **Enable Phishing and Malware protection** and

46

from the same section the user may manage **Security Certificates.** For the **computer wide SSL Settings, the** user may enable **Use SSL 2.0** for trusted websites. We recommend leaving the **Check for server certification revocation** option enabled.

Google Chrome Option Window

- The user can also set **Cookies settings** by choosing the appropriate permission level. For this, expand the **Cookies Setting** fields and select either **Restrict how third-party**

cookies can be used or **Block all cookies** in order to browse in safe mode.

Chapter 6: Free Software Downloads To Protect PC

Many manufacturers offer software downloads for free to protect your computer systems against viruses and spywares. In addition, Microsoft Windows also equips the user with the facility to download free security essential features.

Some of the well-known and trusted software downloads with step-by-step guides are stated below:

Free Edition Of SUPERAntiSpyware

SUPERAntiSpyware Free Edition is an easy to use, free downloading utility and frequently used to remove malicious software on the computer system.

It will take approximately thirty minutes to scan the computer. This process requires that you follow these steps:

- Install SUPERAntiSpyware from the URL **http://www.superantispyware.com/downloadfile.html?productid=SUPERANTISPYWAREFREE**.
- Save the software to an easily accessible location and then double click on the file to launch it.
- In the window which appears, click on the **Next** button and check the option **I Accept**

the License Agreement and again click
Next.
- In the next window that appears, which
  contains the default installation path, click
  Next to start the installation process.
- When the installation is completed, click on the
  Finish button.
- In the next appearing window, click on **Yes** if
  you want the updates.
- Again, click **Next** button until a window with a
  Finish button appears. Then click on the
  Finish button.
- Select the **Protect Home Page**
  (Recommended).
- Click on the **Scan Your Computer** option in
  the main menu window.

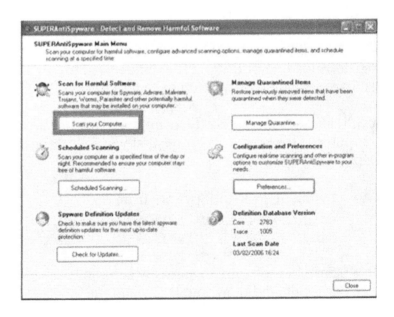

SUPERAntiSpyware Main Menu Window

- Place a dot next to the option **Perform a Complete System Scan** and then select the **Next** button.
- Remove the malicious software that is identified by the anti-spyware program.
- The user can modify **General and Startup settings** according to their needs.

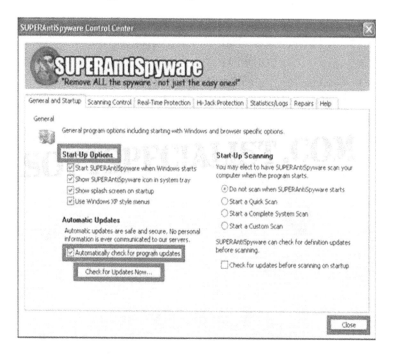

SUPERAntiSpyware Control Center

A-Squared Emsisoft Free Edition

A-Squared Free Edition is an anti-malware application. The A-squared Free Edition is easy to download and can take a maximum of 45 minutes to fix the malware. In addition, it also offers the option of a paid version that has more features.

The following steps are involved for downloading the free edition:

- Visit the A-Squared website at **http://www.emsisoft.com/en/software/free/** for downloading **Emsisoft Free Edition** software.
- Save the file either to your desktop or to any other easily accessed location.
- Double Click the set-up file labeled **a2FreeSetup.exe** and in the opening window select the **Language** for the setup and click **Next.**

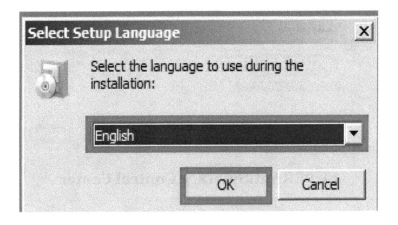

Select Setup Language

- Check the option labeled **I Accept the Agreement** and click on the **Next** button.

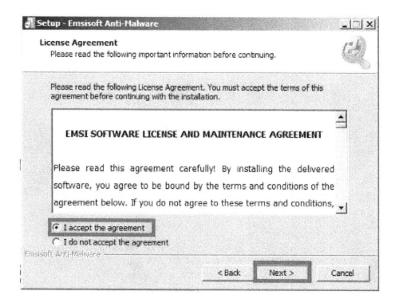

Setup Emsisoft Anti-Malware

- Continue with the default path for installation. For example, it may be **C:\Program Files\a-squared Free.** Then click Next.

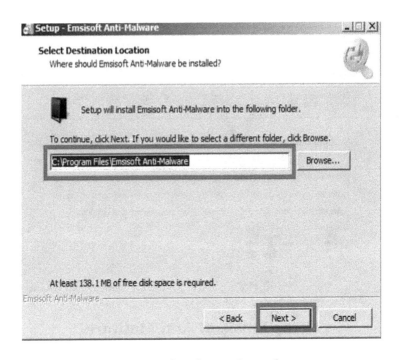

Setup Emsisoft Anti-Malware

- Click on the **Next** button until an **Install** button appears, and then click on the **Install** button.

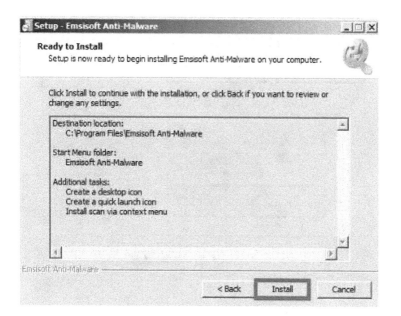

Ready To Install

- After the process of installation is completed, click **Finish** to launch A-Squared software.
- The user can click **Yes** for online updates in the next window.
- Click **Yes** when the A-Squared free edition requests whether you want to restart.
- When the program restarts, Click on the **Scan PC** option.
- Check the option labeled **Deep Scan** to thoroughly scan the hard drive and click on the **Scan** button.

Emsisoft Anti-Malware

- The software will scan for viruses and delete any and all malware it finds.

Note: The user can get more assistance from the website
http://www.emsisoft.com/en/software/antimalware/

Use Online Scanner Panda Nanoscan

Panda Nanoscan is the quickest online available scanner to fix malicious software. This software will consume 5 to 10 minutes to scan the computer scan.

Following steps are involved for the online scan:

- Visit the site http://www.nanoscan.com/ and click on Scan my PC.
- It will request to **install the ActiveX control**. Allow it to install this on your PC.
- The scanner will start loading automatically.

Install Panda Security S.I

- After loading the scanner, it will run **ActiveX.**

Download Active Scan

- Click on the **NanoScan My PC** button and it will give you a list of malwares that is present on your computer system.
- If it detects malware, then identify the path of infection and delete all problematic files.

Note: The Panda store also offers online scan download software named Panda Activescan to fix malicious software. The user can also download the Panda Activescan software to scan his computer from the web link http://www.pandasoftware.com/products/activescan.htm.

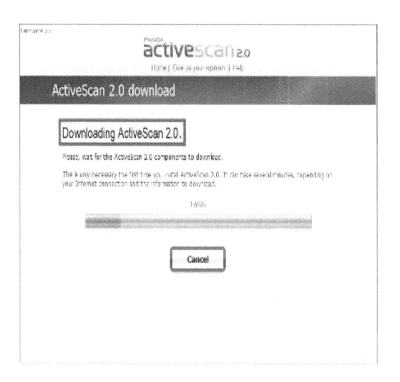

Panda Active Scan

Kaspersky Webscanner

Kaspersky Webscanner is a downloading utility available on the internet to scan computer systems for malicious software. It is also simple to use and takes usually only 1.5 to 2 hours for scanning.

The following steps are required to make use of this utility:

- Download the software from the website.
  http://kaspersky.com/virusscanner.
- **Accept** the license agreement and then you
  will be asked to install **ActiveX control.**
  Continue with downloading ActiveX.

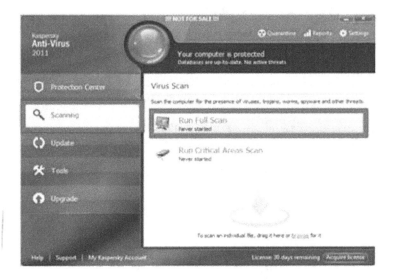

Kaspersky Main Menu Window

- In the next window which appears, select the
  second tab, **Scanning,** from the left pane. On
  the right side, you will see two options. Either
  you want to go for **Run Full Scan** or to select
  the **Run Critical Areas Scan.**
- The scanning process will start and results will
  be displayed to you in the form of a report.

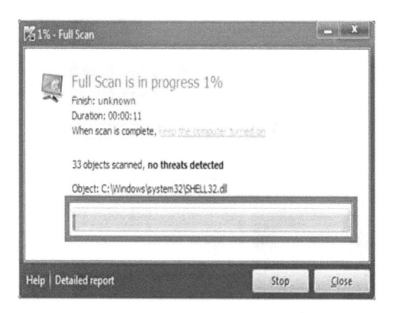

Kaspersky Full Scan Window

- Click the **Save Report As...** option to an
  easily accessible position to access it later on
  for fixing the malware.
- From the third option of **Updates** placed in
  the left pane of main menu window, the user
  can also adjust the settings for regular updates.

Kaspersky Update Window

Employ CCleaner To Eradicate The Malware

CCleaner is a reliable software download available to eliminate viruses and other malicious software.

The following steps are used to employ CCleaner to remove bad software:

- Download **CCleaner** from the website http://www.ccleaner.com/download and

save the file to an easily accessible place on your computer.

- Double click on the setup file named **ccsetup202.exe** and from the opening window, select the **Language.**

CCleaner Setting Window

- Click the option **I agree** to acknowledge the licensing agreement and select the **Next** button.
- Now select the **Install** button to start installation of CCleaner and it completes, click on the **Finish** button.
- Double Click the **CCleaner file icon** on the desktop and from the opening window, click on the **Analyze button.**

CCleaner Main Menu Window

- Now click on **Run Cleaner** to remove all identified malicious files and click **OK** when a warning pop-up appears.
- Select the **Registry** option placed on the left side and from the opening window, click on the Scan for issue button and next click on the Fix Selected Issues option.

CCleaner Registry Integrity Window

- Click **Yes** and save the registry to suitable location.
- Again, click on **Fix all selected issues** option to remove all the malware.

Pocket KillBox

Pocket Killbox is also known for its trustworthiness for deleting corrupt files and folders to protect the computer system.

It is easy to use and requires only a few steps to follow:

- For installing Pocket KillBox, visit the website http://www.killbox.net/ . Click on the **Download** option and then save the software file to an easily accessible place like the desktop.

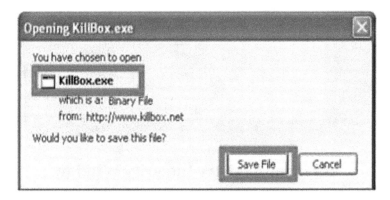

KillBox.exe File Dialog Box

- Double Click on the file killbox.exe to launch it.

- In the opening window, Check the option **Delete on Reboot** and select the **All Files button.**

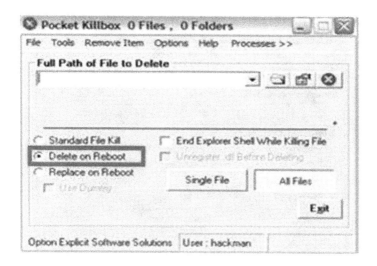

Pocket KillBox

- Enter the path of all the corrupt files in a **Notepad file** and copy all of these paths by selecting all.
- Click on the **File** button and from the drop-down list, select the option **Paste from Clipboard** and click on the **delete file (red and white cross) button.**

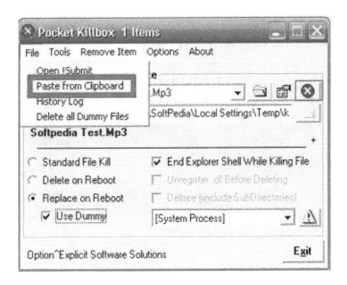

Pocket KillBox Main Menu

- Click **OK** to the Delete on Reboot option.
- The system will **restart** and all the corrupt files will be removed.

LSPFix

If the malicious software has damaged the internet connection, then in that situation, we recommend using LSPFix software to rebuild the connection.

It is simple to use and small enough in size to be fitted in a floppy drive or CD.

It requires following these steps:

- Download the **LSPFix** application from the website http://www.cexx.org/Ispfix.htm and save the file to the desktop.

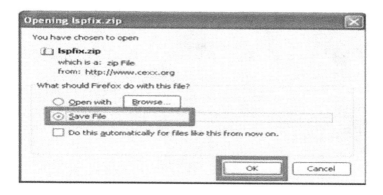

Saving LSPFix File

- Enable the option labeled I know what I'm doing (or enjoy re-installing my operating system....).

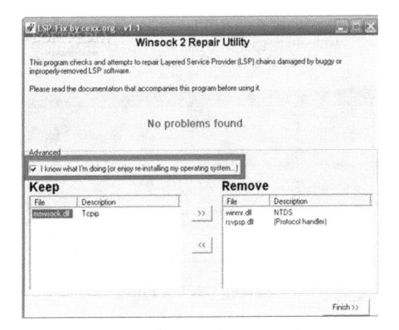

LSP-Fix Main Menu Window

- Identify the corrupt files and carefully move them from the **Keep** section to the **Remove** section with the help of << and >> buttons placed between both the sections.

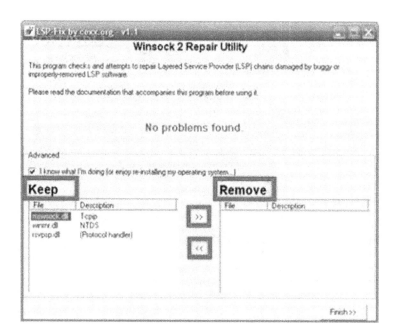

LSPFix Repair Utility Window

- Later on, click on the **Finish** button; you will be presented with a Repair Summary dialog box.

Repair Summary

- Finally, **Reboot** the computer system.

Other Suggested Software

In this day and age, dozens of free anti-virus downloads are available to fix malicious software. Apart from the above-mentioned software downloads, the user may install any of the software mentioned below from their respective given website addresses, or can find them by entering the key words in some search engines:

AVG Anti-Virus Free Edition

Website Address:
http://www.pcworld.com/downloads/file/fi d,15202-order,1/description.html

McAfee FreeScan

Website Address:
http://www.pcWorld.com/downloads/file/f
id,22921-order,1/description.html

Avast! Free Edition

Website Address:
http://www.pcWorld.com/downloads/file/f
id,64535-order,1/description.html

AVG Anti-Rootkit

Website Address:
http://www.pcworld.com/downloads/file/fi
d,65198-order,1/description.html

Chapter 7: Paid Software To Protect Computer Systems

Although numerous free software downloads are available to protect computer systems, many of them are not trustworthy or capable enough to ensure ultimate protection. So many vendors are also offering featured and compatible paid software subscription packages. The user can download this software from the internet.

Some of these are listed below:

Panda Subscription Packages

The Panda store also offers many other paid software options in different yearly subscription packages for fixed terms, like Panda Internet Security 2011 and Panda Antivirus Pro 2011. The user can get the online subscription from the website address: http://www.pandasoftware.com/products/activescan.htm.

Panda Product Line

Folder Password Expert

Folder Password Protect is highly reliable software to protect folders from unauthorized and illegal access. It is available in a monthly subscription package for $39.95. It has the ability to provide password protection from the internal hard disk to external hard drives like memory cards, USBs, etc.

It is easy to use and involves only a few steps to get it working. The user can subscribe to this security software from the website http://www.folder-password-expert.com/.

Folder Password Expert Window

BitDefender Antivirus Pro 2011

BitDefender is another featured anti-virus download available online to fix viruses and malware. Its subscription is available on $39.95 for a whole year and it supports multiple configuration options.

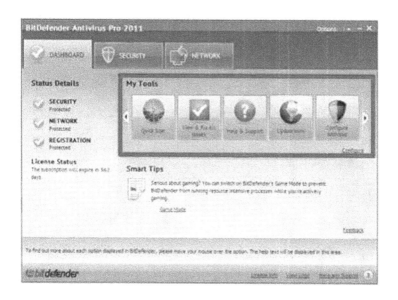

BitDefender Antivirus Pro 2011

BullGuard Antivirus

BullGuard has also been called the most superb anti-malware of 2011 by IT experts. It has an extraordinarily effective spam filter and its yearly subscription is available at a rate of $29.95.

Install Double Anti-Spy Professional v2

This program is also highly rated anti-malware software, and is available in a package for

$29.00/year. It is ranked as one of the best softwares on the market for fixing malware.

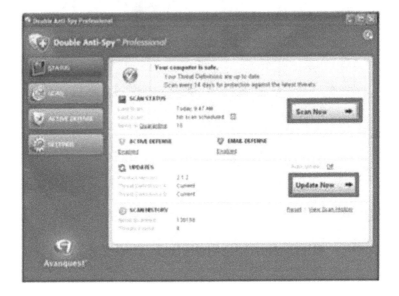

Double Anti-Spy Professional

List Of Some Of The Other Paid Softwares:

The user may employ some other featured and paid packages of anti-malware from the list below. Their website addresses can be found on the internet by entering the listed key words in a search engine.

- eScan Anti-Virus 11
- F-Secure Anti-Virus 2011
- G Data Anti-Virus
- Norton Antivirus

- Outpost Antivirus Pro 7.0

Conclusion

Today, the spread of malicious software is growing faster than ever. That fact leads to the need to develop anti-malware software with the same rapid pace. Although Microsoft Windows offers many built-in utilities and online services to protect your computer systems, these are not sufficient to defend against all the possible malicious activities.

The new level of threat demands the regular use of highly featured and updated software that is available in both paid and free versions. The set of tactics and tips mentioned in this guide will help the user to set a suitable defense against viruses, spyware and malware.

Recommended Resources

- HowExpert.com – Quick 'How To' Guides on All Topics from A to Z by Everyday Experts.
- HowExpert.com/free – Free HowExpert Email Newsletter.
- HowExpert.com/books – HowExpert Books
- HowExpert.com/courses – HowExpert Courses
- HowExpert.com/clothing – HowExpert Clothing
- HowExpert.com/membership – HowExpert Membership Site
- HowExpert.com/affiliates – HowExpert Affiliate Program
- HowExpert.com/writers – Write About Your #1 Passion/Knowledge/Expertise & Become a HowExpert Author.
- HowExpert.com/resources – Additional HowExpert Recommended Resources
- YouTube.com/HowExpert – Subscribe to HowExpert YouTube.
- Instagram.com/HowExpert – Follow HowExpert on Instagram.
- Facebook.com/HowExpert – Follow HowExpert on Facebook.